"Many years ago, when I first traveled through Yellow Springs, Ohio, the home of Antioch College, I felt a strange *Twilight-Zone* presence in that Sunday-morning vacant town. The inn's proprietor was not surprised because "upstairs Rod Serling taught class." I felt the vibe. Now, I'm catching that vibe again with Rikki Santer's *Stopover*, her poetic riffs on Sterling's *Twilight Zone*, which takes the series to another dimension, where the allegories are soft reminders of our humanity, our vulnerability, and our innocence. Our enjoyment is seeing episodes with "no moral, no message, no prophetic tract/just a suit of armor held together by one bolt/call it faith." She soars, for instance, when she shares the bird's-eye view of Mickey Rooney as a washed-up jockey, condensing the aging loser in a prison-like room with "walls closing in as your consonants rattled, your character out of his mind with shortness, neon gel of your ranting, nighty night." Rikki and Rod parse the lonely life of a has-been: Rod's washed-up jockey and Rooney's seedy actor with "frayed pockets: king high, ace low." In her cento poem, she uses Serling's voice in a fantastic world full of question marks and leavened by the possibility but never the reality of bromides. Rikki Santer's poetic appreciation of *The Twilight Zone* series embraces for our consideration cynicism about our intentions and unconditional love for our imperfection. Enter her lyrical zone to enjoy Serling's simple tales as the stuff of poetry. If you think humankind to be masterfully in charge, then Rikki and Rod will remind you that we are doomed to be served on a platter by those who know we deserve it."

   —John DeSando, producer and host of *It'sMovie Time* and *Cinema Classics* as well as podcasts *Back Talk* and *Double Take* for NPR's WCBE 90.5 FM, Columbus, Ohio.

"Fifty years ago, Rod Serling appeared as a stylistic voice of a mundane angel, "…offering for our consideration…" melodramas with undertones of Kierkegaard and Socrates. Thematically *The Twilight Zone* was a freakish variety of episodes dwelling between irony, despair, and commercial sponsors delivered one evening a week. The peripatetic poet Rikki Santer provides a similar episodic world that like the form of the Sixties television show, frames a just beyond the narrator's voice. For those of us who were fans of the program, an allusion to Rod Serling's, monochromatic, nearly monotonal signaled the immanent appearance of absurdity; we all heard him introducing some moment of our private chaos. Santer's poems in *Stopover* allude to that conscious landscape that grows irony and paradox. She incorporates a variety of poetic forms employing a Modernist lens with Post Modern appropriations: ghazals, refractions of pop songs, cinquains, centos, how-to articles and imaginary auditions. Readers will find her celebrating an aspect of poetic humanity within a philosophical apprecition like Serling's characters, simultaneously oblivious and acutely engaged with the contextual minutiae of awareness. In the twilit world of these poems, overlooked witnesses testify. Emily Dickinson appears, along with Boone's Farm wine, Carol Burnett, badly costumed Martians, antisemitic suburban parents, Buster Keaton and even a crossword elegy for Eddie Van Halen. Like the pernicious guile of Rod Serling, these aren't poems to pass an evening, but rather strange songs that sting and undercut the notions of nostalgia and societal innocence. This is the cold eye of the passing horseman. Readers should not mistake her enthusiastic language for a showy gush of technique; these dimmed down epiphanies are more like the breaths of air of a woman struggling not to drown. Rikki Santer is the mistress of misdirection, forcing the reader to look where they only believe they are choosing to look---but instead exactly where she desires their vision to be."

—D E Zuccone, author of *Vanishes*

STOPOVER

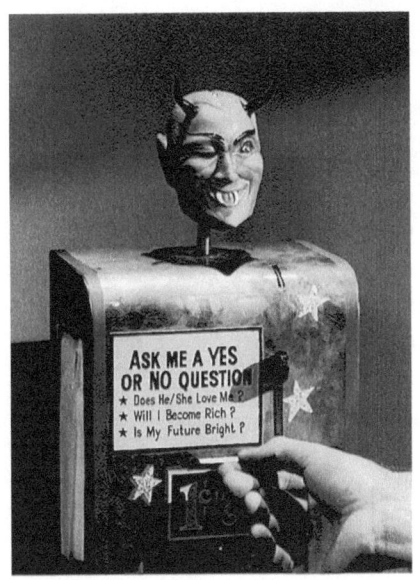

Poems by Rikki Santer

Luchador Press
Big Tuna, TX

Copyright © Rikki Santer, 2021
First edition 1 3 5 7 9 10 8 6 4 2
ISBN: 978-1-952411-74-8
LCCN: 2021945678

Front cover image: Marc Alan Ross
All rights reserved. No part of this publication may be reproduced or transmitted in any form or by any means, electronic or mechanical, including photocopying, recording or by info retrieval system, without prior written permission from the author.

Special thanks to the editors of these publications:

Arc Magazine : "In Which Obsolete Tries to Rewrite Its Story: The Lost Episode," *Atherton Review*: "Turkeys We Love," *Black Moon*: "First Offering," "Last Offering," *Blood & Bourbon*: "Art of Being Human," *Citron Review*: "Gift Shop at the Museum of Fear," *Creosote* : "Black Moon, Gray Card," *Dissonance Magazine* : "How to Tame a Dream," *Eastern Iowa Review* : "Dear Twilight Zone Episode Starring Me," *Gyroscope Review* : "Cento for His Monologues," *Indolent Books (Transition: Poems in the Afterglow)* : "Breach," *The Klecksograph* : "Ventriloquist's Oath," *LOL Comedy* : "Annoyed Aliens," *Pink Plastic House* : "Crown of Cinquains for the Women of Twilight Zone," *Pudding Magazine* : "Chiaroscuro Eye Candy All Day," "Some Crossword Clues" *The Ravens Perch* : "Consider," *Remington Review* : "Emily Dickinson Auditions to Host *Twilight Zone*," *Rough Cut Press*: "Suburban Trajectory," *Rusty Truck* : "New Year's Eve, at the Handoff with *Twilight Zone*," *Silver Birch Press* : "Stopover," *SLAB* : "Coin," *Slant* : "Phantom Camera," *Sledgehammer* : "Zones," *Synchronized Chaos Magazine* : "Detours," "Poetry Accessories," "Rod Serling Takes a Stab at Stand Up," *Tomorrow and Tomorrow* : "Enchanted Things," "Twilight Ghazal," *Twin Pies Literary Journal* : "Solitaire"

Also by Rikki Santer:

Front Nine: A Biography of Place ; *Clothesline Logic* ; *Fishing for Rabbits* ; *Khahiki Redux* ; *Make Me That Happy* ; *Dodge, Tuck, Roll* ; *In Pearl Broth* ; *Drop Jaw* ; *Head to Toe of It* ; *How to Board a Moving Ship*

I am grateful for the gracious attention of the editors who first published the poems that appear in this collection.

I also offer deep gratitude to the generous poets in my life who offered their guidance in the critiquing of these poems: Sayuri Ayers, Steve Abbott, Kathleen Burgess, Sandy Feen, Jennifer Hambrick, Susann Moeller, Linda Fuller-Smith, Chuck Salmons, Rose Smith, Mark Webb, and all my Bistro and Salon colleagues.

Also, thank you to my gifted friends, Steve Abbott, John Burroughs, John DeSando, and Dom Zuccone, for their thoughtful and artful words of support via book blurbs. It's an honor to have your words join mine.

Thank you, Jason Ryberg of Luchador Press for so deftly shepherding this manuscript to publication and for once again, believing in my work.

Thank you, Rod Serling, for your vision, and the legacy you left for generations.

And how lucky I am to have my favorite artist of all time in my back pocket. Thank you, Marc Ross, for a stunning cover and a lifetime of love together.

Author's Note:

During these trying times of pandemic and deep divide in our country, it has been my reprieve to binge in the moral dexterity of *The Twilight Zone*. Many of these poems are boxed like the Magnavox television screen of my youth, the original messenger for a five-season anthology series that lasted from 1959-1964. For any readers who are newcomers to the original series—**spoiler alert**—iconic, twist endings are herein honored. All episode references appear at the end of this collection.

TABLE OF CONTENTS

New Year's Eve, at the Handoff with Twilight Zone

Chiaroscuro Eye Candy All Day / 1

First Offering / 2

Detours / 3

Suburban Trajectory / 5

Consider / 6

Twilight Ghazal / 7

Enchanted Things / 8

Rod Serling Takes a Stab at Stand-Up / 10

Turkeys We Love / 13

Zones / 15

Stopover / 18

Annoyed Aliens / 19

Crown of Cinquains for Women of *Twilight Zone* / 21

Emily Dickinson Auditions to Host / 23

Ventriloquist's Oath / 25

Phantom Camera / 26

Some Crossword Clues / 27

Solitaire / 29

Poetry Accessories / 30

How To Tame a Dream / 31

Breach / 32

In Which Obsolete Tries to Rewrite Its Story:
The Lost Episode / 33

Dear Twilight Zone Episode Starring Me / 34

Gift Shop at the Museum of Fear / 35

Black Moon, Gray Card / 36

Coin / 37

Last Offering / 39

Art of Being Human / 40

Cento for His Monologues / 42

EPISODE REFERENCES / 45

*Where are we, Bob? Where **are** we?*

>—Millie from "Stopover in a Quiet Town"
>(Season 5, Episode 30)

There is nothing in the dark that isn't there when the lights are on.

>—Rod Serling

New Year's Eve, At the Handoff With Twilight Zone

> *Rod Serling will be there to greet us once more with*
> *the annual New Year's "Twilight Zone" marathon on*
> *SYFY beginning December 31 at 6 am.*

Yearful tearfuls of days swirl away like moths in the night
and I find myself still orbiting without a reliable storyline so
I tune into the next 24 hours of tooth & claw in this other
dimension that pokes at my ears with its four-note motif of
crawly dissonance & dangerous bongos. The slip & slide of
binge, each two-act shadow box skitters after that spot in my
mind where Breton claimed contradiction surrenders, each
supernatural chamber piece a funhouse mirror, endurance
run that forgives for a while my Whack-A-Mole life.

Chiaroscuro Eye Candy All Day

Praise sweaty close-ups and angular croppings that keep us fed in reruns. Praise puppet theater of inner torment for subjects suspended above brutal irony of precipice. Praise auteur host whose confident hands clasp at crotch level. Praise his chiseled face that deepens into even-more-handsomeness through bare-boned allure of black & white. Praise shadows that broker light for losers & dreamers, and tight tight compositions that carry them across the infinity of living room. Praise wild universe pulsing in zeitgeist vortex of monochrome. Praise two-word, five-season moniker, oh ye of existential buzzword. Praise warped & twisted noir in episodic containers, each brimming with rapid unraveling then the snap back, delicious whirls of switcheroo.

First Offering

> *On 10/2/59 the first episode of Twilight Zone.*
> *"Where is Everybody?" was broadcast on CBS.*

We are a frightened breed that begins our lives in canted angle, each life's arc just another pilot episode that will leave us with a last breath to question where IS everybody? We are sailing stones inscribing tracks across the comeuppance of empty sidewalks. Mannequins fall for us, smoldering cigars monogram our tongues, phone booths encase us with impotent numbers, church bells sear. We hope ice cream will save us, the tic tac toes of solitaire in the dirt, yet typical results seldom vary in the mirror's cold echo. We can't seem to wake from the box in the hangar. We can't seem to manufacture a different way out.

Detours

Couple bottles of Boone's Farm that Belinda's older brother got for us at A & C Beverage when we met up with him around the corner and of course the peyote buttons and we were off cruising country backroads in my mom's '63 Impala convertible that last summer night after graduation when we found a moist valley of fireflies that swallowed us like the sparkling, star-filled sky as if we entered a Kusama Infinity Mirror when time was giving us a second chance to lose ourselves before maturity showed up with handcuffs and magicked the key away.

Midnight phantom footfall inside the bedroom ceiling and the scene dissolves out of focus and then into focus again landing me in that prickly flip of past, not to repair history in order to save a Joan of Arc or Soulika sister, but to squirm into my middle school locker so that this time Ruth White won't find me with her punches when I take the last chocolate pudding cup in the cafeteria before she can get her spoon-ringed fingers around it.

A jet stream snares me, squeezes me through jalousie window slats to territory of bigger/faster/more/more/more instead of snailing through sweaty lines of government cheese and unemployment. How to make doppelgänger sense of it, these roundabout visits that send me rewinding to never meet up with Gus who stained me with a hickey he claimed was the size of a whale's.

How can I be my best ingredient, in glory to each birthday's butter cream? To follow the next trail of twine through hallways where Easter eggs are painted zygotes and that if I swallow one, I could clear my throat of trouble.

Suburban Trajectory

do you remember the time I sat at your parents' polished mahogany table in their crystal dining room while they whispered about me in their gleaming kitchen with a marble island way bigger than my mother's apartment kitchenette and I thought I heard *wayward upbringing* and *Jesus killers* before they joined us with their strained smiles and heaping platter of breakfast bacon or at the cafeteria's lunch table when the unwrapping of my matzo peanut butter sandwich made my ligaments twitch in the crosshairs of all your smirking eyes or your *kike kike kikes* in so many different high school bathrooms yet the shame was for my suburban sheltering like when in the back of a college classroom during a lecture on Celan I dissolved from my body to the ragged stench of a Dachau barracks death ship and among the sunken faces was mine and then I returned to find each of you staring at my tear-stained cheeks so in this category of my making I've been led by a trail angel to find myself circumnavigated by the guilt that lives in luck to remind myself of the tattoo buried deep into the flesh of my Hebrew school teacher's arm as it danced before her eager chalkboard

Consider

When you consider a pitch to end all pitches—a pitch for angels some say—what materializes in the dusty corners of your apartment will be a pitch *as delicate as Shantung Silk carried across ocean in satchels underneath the ruby throats of birds,* then your perfumed scarf will touch down upon a vestibule's tapestry rug and proclaim your final exit. How euphemisms spiral into themselves as our pendulums slow, and cantankerous static clings to our nose hairs. How we want to chew the date off our ticket to the Imperial Lounge and just keep rolling around the lush cornfield where we were wished, *olly olly oxen free.* How we yearn to get drunk on cocktails of instant smiles and cellular serums, our pinkies tapping our lips. How we limit, to a parakeet mirror, our scavenger hunts for wrinkles and dearly pay to have done what alchemists do with plastic. Death will launch the trajectory of our accumulating selfies and leave us with our monkey minds gobsmacked like *undigested bits of beef.* So wag your tongue all you want at that grandfather clock and swathe your phone in a crochet shawl to muffle calls from the grave. Branch shadows will play upon your sleeping face, and your scarab ring, too loose now for your fingers, will twang to the floor. No such place as exactly what happened.

Twilight Ghazal

In creases where Storyteller opens sky to hindsight,
riddle is spooned into dusky stew of twilight.

Rhythms of our bodies slow and surrender,
held in the silvery arms of trickster twilight.

Garble of neon night flashes its fonts in zones,
launched by pulsing capillaries of twilight.

Wooden phone booths inside crowded bars—
conveyors for what haunts in tissue of twilight.

Stars—spinning blades to whittle what we don't know
we need, helixes steamed with seduction of twilight.

Enchanted Things
after Talking Heads

You may find yourself trying on a dead man's two-tone loafers—stylish missiles to take you back to sooty alleys, tequila shots with sugar cubes, borrowed revenge. Ebony? Onyx? Licorice? Black olive? How many shades of pooling blood can ooze from your noir crayon?

Anchor of question, arrows of answers, another cup of quandary at the threshold. Does paranormal have a to-do list? Squads of deep mirrors everywhere—cracked, rearviewed or doubled, convex or cobwebbed, each distorts who's right around your corner. How many times can your reflection shatter until it's released?

You may find yourself quivering in the thrall of a sizzling herd of mannequins. What does matter hum to a spirit sporting nylon pigtails and marble eyeballs? You may find yourself entwined by the twitching muscles of homebound. Over there, tail of your electric shaver slithers down the stairway. Over there, typewriter keys in dizzy beat with castanets armed and vengeful. Negotiate Oedipal trappings with your toy telephone. Chew on greedy slices from a camera that browns your future like a toaster. Gravel dust cakes under your fingernails once you're spotted by goggle eyes of death car.

How well can you redecorate when you move into the innards of an antique radio? Your piano in the parlor speaks slot machine. Patch of moonlight fevers ivories. Now you're melancholy miniature cozying up to a 19th century dollhouse damsel. Raise your pitch at the end of your statements and *voilà* you've invented questions. A gold thimble from the lost floor of a department store, ever so much fun in the chill wind?

You may ask yourself how many tangents can you add to a tangent? What's in-between and out-of-bounds? Marvelous gimmick, once ancient anagram of magic. To fetishize square pegs. To net silver fish in twilight.

Rod Serling Takes a Stab at Stand Up

Before he says anything he draws deep
on a fresh Chesterfield and turns his head

to profile so he can better think sideways.
Swish pan / swish pan / swish pan / ah,

there's the ringmaster, hot light, hot mic
and he's rapier thin cool in a black mohair

3 roll 2 sack suit and crispy white oxford
spread collar. *Glad you all could make it tonight*

*because you're traveling now with the best
dressed man in any dimension.* Rod straightens

his Brooks Brothers double stripe and clenches
his jaw for the baritone glide. *I just flew into*

*town an hour ago and boy, are my gremlins
tired.* Rod straddles a stool. *You know, some*

*people call me the Arthur Miller of science
fiction TV, but my wife calls me television's*

*Groucho Marx of eyebrows... Yeah, I'm a
Jewish kid born on December 25, that one*

*Christmas Day my parents had something else
delivered besides Chinese take out.* He grips

the mic and a beam of light launches off his
silver military bracelet. *You might have*

*heard I was a paratrooper during WW2,
but hell, that wasn't half as harrowing as*

*battling with TV sponsors... I'm no dummy
but we all know what it is to look into the face*

*of the Twilight Zone—you have to have toilet
paper with you at all times for the doo-doo-*

*doo-doo... But seriously, I do hold the record for
winning 6 Emmys in outstanding writing for a*

*drama series but what the hell do those two aliens
in the front row care. They've probably got better*

*jokes on their planet, like"an Earthling and a Martian
walk into a diner"...* A mound of ash has been softly

growing near his Florsheims. *My daughters keep
telling me that I smoke too many cigarettes, but then*

*I remind them of our digs in Pacific Palisades and
Cayuga Lake, and they stop nagging me. Oh yeah,*

Sometimes I like playing the "In Rod We Trust" card.
Rod drops his cigarette butt to the floor and rubs it

out with his shoe. *So that's my time, folks. I'm heading
back home now to the hacienda and when I get there,*

*I'll walk into my study, sit down, put paper in the typewriter,
fix the margins, turn the paper up, and bleed.*

Turkeys We Love

An aging silent movie clown, married to his childhood
        sweetheart—aka, the subjunctive mood—skitters
down a dusty road, sifting through chickens and pigs that
        tease his ankles. It's late 19th century flirting with

early 1960s and it's not what a comedian can do for you, but
        what you can do for a comedian. Buster Keaton,
dour in pork pie, journeys across time in gizmo helmet
        without his pants *(I hung 'em up in 1890)* to land in

another sovereign state of deadpan with fading, acrobatic
        feats of hijinks. *Just watch your step, Mulligan*, as he
leaves behind punchlines on intertitles and navigates
        set pieces in his newfangled hometown, a modern

America that celebrates slick TV men who don't have all
        their buttons. And then there's perennial sidekick
Andy Devine with raspy, rat-a-tat-tatting escapades launching
        through the homespun gap in his teeth.

Endearing blowhard until Martians believe him, but his whiny
        harmonica is too much for alien kidnappers and it's
back to the general store where cronies laugh off his tale as
        just another Frisby cry for a confabulating wolf. And

what about those two Agneses claiming their ether
>of comedy? A 60s Siri called greatest mind of the century,
yet out of her mind. Computer femme fatale who likes entrapping
>white-coated men with her flirty knobs and winking lights

in a sanitized suite. Most perfect casting of nerd-chiseled
>Wally Cox, too timid for a girlfriend, too unhinged
for a tantrum of paper tongues spewing messages of *Venus
>Schmee-nus*. And then the other Miss Agnes—Carol

Burnett's overbite ensures her ingenue awkwardness while her
>guardian angel, Jesse White, zaps down from the heavenly
vault of 3rd Celestial Division to chomp on a wet cigar and
>deliver a sugary fable. Comic relief or comic grief? Yes, corny

thickets, gnarly and sluggish, but still classic with room tones of
>funny, like Izzy, my sweet, sappy uncle, who holds joyous
court each evening in the crowded dining hall of his dingy nursing
>home on the outskirts of Queens.

Zones

flashlight off the shelf
   through the woods
      inside the cave
         spotlight under chin
            warps
               twists
                  distorts
                  disturbs
                     snaps back

                       submitted
                       for your consideration
                shut your eyes
                for wishes errant
                for frame shifters
                for deep-dished what if
   what next
   what now

just who are the people you nod
   your hellos to

I'm Talking Tina
>   and I'm going to kill you

how thin the line
> between real and mind
>> how thin the plug
>>> that drains clarity
>>>> the shell around brutality
>>>>> the answer why
>>>>>> the memory of Earth
>>>>>>> the cool hand
>>>>>>>> to brush
>>>>>>>>> over tired eyes

>>>>>> find the zipper
>>>>> in the gremlin's suit
>>>> without our masks
>>>> we are caricatures
>>> cannonaded by lies
>>> shelled by insecurity
>> straddled by humiliation
>> targeted by isolation
>>> blown clean apart

    living in dead run
        no salvation signpost
            up ahead
        clocks
        made by earthlings
            something else
                created time

Stopover

Drop me off somewhere in suburban Ohio where nostalgia conjures me with a topaz wand. Not hometown, instead call it tabernacle where a front yard cloak of dogwood blossoms stands in for the whole, where tame childhood in peach gingham thrills whenever concrete mixer truck in stripedchurn rattles past the playground, where glint of Girl Scout compass nestles in Mill Creek silt. Yet on bedroom wall a doe-eyed Keane reminds that timidity is a false-bottomed boat. Black Leather Jacket forces finger fuck in a tufted field behind the school. Terrier's neck snaps broken in a neighbor's backyard. Suicide note on dresser, feet sway like the tongue of a bell. Memory blows on ashes to scatter them—give & take.

Annoyed Aliens

      detest the fodder
of looking like some of us—
Martian zookeepers in Roman togas,
Marlon Brando wannabes,
three-eyed, three-armed invaders
who plot over bad coffee in
out-of-the-way diners.

Irritated aliens
whine about reruns,
tired jokes like
did you hear the one
about the two-headed Martian
who walks into a dump full of barflies
then flutters its jerry-rigged antennas
to turn actor grit into slapstick?
And it doesn't make it any better
when they're joined
by twin-boy Venusians
who shimmy in with pencil
mustaches and crotchety
voices of grown men.

But what really ticks them off
are swollen Kanamit craniums
of cookbook authors
(we probably taste like chicken)
and those turtle-necked,
slick-suited, white-gloved
no-mouths, who get
played by a blues-harped
blowhard from Pitchville.

Aggrieved aliens believe
we should own up to our
what-any-other-looks-like.
Therein lies
our humanoid's tale,
inflatable,
deflatable,
and viscid at best.

Crown of Cinquains for Women of *Twilight Zone*

Beauty
in Mercury
Montclair, beckoned by a
scarecrow man with crucible thumb,
Scythe's fruit.

    Past her
prime but what is
prime but that which she wraps
in celluloid shrine for her own
heaven.

    She with
only grunts, moans,
tiny toy robot rays,
her dull knife, hatchet, hovel=
giant.

    Beauty
haunted by bus
station doppelgänger,
Mona Lisa smirk in a
mirror.

                        Behold
clucking doctor,
woman as ready wound,
mummified face waiting, fable
unwrapped.

Emily Dickinson Auditions to Host

There is a fifth dimension,
>*that hovered there awhile*

beyond that which is known to man
>*only the Chemist can disclose.*

It is a dimension as vast as space
>*Be not expressed by Suns alone*

and as timeless as infinity
>*From Blank to Blank*
>*A Threadless Way.*

It is in the middle ground between light and shadow,
>*For Pattern is the Mind bestowed*

between science and superstition,
>*The Feet, mechanical, go round*

and it lies between the pit of man's fears
>*As if a Goblin with a Gauge*

and the summit of his knowledge
>*The Finite - furnished*
>*With the Infinite.*

This is the dimension of imagination
>*The Brain is wider than the sky*

It is an area which we call the Twilight Zone
>*So huge, so hopeless to conceive.*

You're traveling through another dimension,
> *as twilight long begun*

a dimension not only of sight and sound but of mind
> *The Brain is deeper than the sea.*

A journey into a wondrous land
> *The creatures chuckle on the roofs*

whose boundaries are that of imagination.
> *And we look farther on.*

That's the signpost up ahead -
> *Fearless - the cobweb swings from the ceiling*

your next stop, the Twilight Zone
> *Might I but moor - tonight -*
> *In thee!*

Ventriloquist's Oath
for Little Caesar and Willie

Check each hollow head for explosives, even they can have minds of their own. Toss your vaudeville voice from trunk to trunk, forge double gestalt with your sureshot tongue. Tumble through each second-rate shanty nightclub routine with brash block of wood, bottle of hooch. Button up each wayward planet into your box of tricks, but always be beside yourself for any object that longs to be co-conspirator. Even rocks talk ancient language.   Shut your mouth & listen up.

Phantom Camera
after Jaswinder Bolina

How to square it, lost and almost empty
in my mother's Chevy Impala convertible
that multiple sclerosis took too early from her—
mood ring impotent in the glove compartment,
spoke wheel covers rusted and bent.
Up ahead another gravity angle
and the shaggy dog that lives inside me
whimpering I should have done more.
I yearn to be a minor character
but up ahead a nursing home bedroom,
her only room for almost a decade.
The lilac box of it, the lavender cell of it,
where waiting optioned her life. Her crated
radio scripts we should have read aloud together,
my weekly phone calls that should have been daily.
Up ahead, blue skies in black & white. I walk
into town on what her legs wished they could have been—
for a cheeseburger deluxe, strawberry milkshake,
and a blank book of mathematical formulas
to reassemble atoms for the way
we want them to be.

Some Crossword Clues
for Eddie Van Halen (1955-2020)

Westerns always throw their nets over me, ever since those weekly nights in Dodge City with *Gun Smoke* and my dad. He was a softy for Festus and Kitty while I remained fixated on the perfect slouch of a scruffy marshal's hat and the dancing beauty mark of a sanitized whore. Enter *Twilight Zone*. #3 down—the four-letter name for that Doomsday peddler who deals in everything: Henry J. F A T E, a fanciful little man in a black frock coat who offers each of us his elixir—either climb out of the pit or fall into one. I was lucky. My saloon was a sunny kitchen with swinging doors and shots of Nestle's Quik. I spent hot summers getting my cowgirl on, prancing in my homespun shirt with eyes painted on my eyelids. # 7 across—how many seconds, in three letters, for paternal accuracy: it took T E N for Dad to lift me atop my favorite stallion on the carousel, its gaping mouth muted with teeth bared. #12 down—a three-letter forbidden boyfriend, G U S, pulling up in a cloud of smoke, legs spread wide on his BSA Thunderbolt to take me on a ride for lukewarm beer and a hand of providence. #15 across—I was never really tough; I was more like eleven letters worth of M A R S H M A L L O W, yet I never did take kindly to the lethargy and phony-baloney of my hometown. Whenever I got into a heap of trouble I'd call in #20 down—three-letters of stunt man in my big mustached brother, R O Y, whose real name was Wesley but he fancied himself a cowpoke rancher humming *Happy Trails* for his sound track. On this mournful day in autumn, Van Halen's *joke-'em-if-they-can't-take-a-fuck harmonies* of that tune loop truer. Across, down, what's the difference. Adios, sweet Eddie. You were the shredding hombre who showed us what magic dirt could do.

Solitaire

for Mickey Rooney and his one-man performance,
"Last Night of a Jockey"

In the paradise of remembering, you begin nestled and sparkling in that last clearing of Shakespeare's enchanted forest, *No more yielding but a dream.* Puck's uppity nose yours for a lifetime. Your kazoo-voiced kid with stars & stripes in a comic-strip grin, five-foot-two, song-joke-dance-man polish, big box-office draw now wailing in a run-down box of a room Serling made just for you, pint-sized prince *rounding the far turn and coming up fast on the rail.* Rage, grief, searing self-loathing, you played it straight, gristled the phone's receiver, each shiny object a painful mirror, walls closing in as your consonants rattled, your character out of his mind with shortness, neon gel of your ranting, nighty night, thunderstorm, then awakened to your feet dangling off the foot of the bed and you, cowed by the cackling of a slicked-back, suited alter-ego into a ten-foot Stretch Armstrong now jockeyed out of jockeydom, this one-man episode, your acting chops in blazing, raw bravura. Your legacy complex: Lothario & Gambler & Victim of Elder Abuse which is to say a *Hollywood Train Wreck* when at 93 you ended your tableau with frayed pockets: king high, ace low.

Poetry Accessories

spurs of moment + tertiary motivation + worn copy of *Ye Book of Ye Dark Arts* that flies off top shelf + riddle for riddling + doodle for doodling + fecund uncertainty + that crazy moon + blacks, whites & grays spring-loaded + quill pen at attention + ti-tle/act/scene/cup-inside-cup-inside-cup mash-ups from Brother Will + sand conjured from your loafers + first picture book cherished + porcelain tureen with footnotes brimming + six-foot hot dog bun for napping under stars + dust motes whirling in sunbeam + pixel by pixel hearing + gaze unmediated & gliding + cockles squirming your heart + Harpo's harp in barbed wire + Méliès's flash, dazzle & poof + world too small to be satisfying + horsepower via head-stone + *va va voom* + *ipsy dipsy* + *za za zoom*

How to Tame a Dream

You miss the soothing slip into sleep as TV snow static wrapped you in tomorrow's callback. The night contained you in a safe frame where sails filled and your ship began to dip into orbit, coiling and liquid. But tonight, like most nights, frigid is sweltering and torrid is frostbite. When you tumble backwards, your head snaps forward in time to save you. You wake bone still. Camera pans up to a torn gown of stars. You weigh your inventory. They say *a dream takes only a second or so, yet in that second a person can live a lifetime.* If you can't forgive the brutal carnival, then perchance forgive the glistening leopard spots that lured you. If you can't retrieve all your marbles lost under the fruit cocktail tree, then perchance retrieve the molten moonlight arguing with darkness. If you tunnel in, through bite-sized chapters to the other side of recurring, you may slow down the gnawing of your feverish nightmares and find yourself tangled not strangled by a grayscale rainbow mid-frayed or a mammal's searching tongue, long and velvet.

Breach

after Trump supporters stormed the Capitol 1/6/21

the news breaking us again//again
and if they are angry give them objects for their anger
perception of perception
still locked in the purgatory of 2020
but most of all you will make this mob an extension of your self
curry the physics of armed herds braying
at the God door for more dopamine hits from a viral internet
fingering the hilts of their swords
in a country of darkdark Maple Streets
with not enough justice to mete out
for crackpot theories bubbling in cauldrons
and then one morning the country woke up from underneath
   its sleep
monoliths on the hate spectrum
what can cure us of these lunatic pleasures

In Which Obsolete Tries to Rewrite Its Story: The Lost Episode

Master shot:
Tall doors loom open
to black matte walls, room almost
empty except for a long narrow table
and a towering obelisk of a lectern.

Chancellor speaks:
It's been 5,000 years of the zero game;
once nothing appears, it's here to stay.

Obsolete enters and declares:

a lot of me may not be as bad as a lot of them
but now I am a fable that's lost
its imprint in the ever-shifting ground.
Look over there—musty insides of a language factory.
Look over there—can any of your minds snatch me
from this soup of shadows?

Look over there—over there—Look-
Over-Theres on rewind.

Dear *Twilight Zone* Episode Starring Me

You can always tell by the clouds and today looks like snow but let's start in the middle and cherry-pick points from the Freytag, like my up-and-down crawling supermarket aisles on my knees picking up change that rolled under shelves crowded with condiments and boxed shortcuts. And the first act should also be about how I lie to be kind, especially to department store mannequins because my boyfriend is hard to love, but so am I because being personable is exhausting. There's got to be lots of mirrors: at the garden trellis, on my bedroom ceiling, in the mailbox to double its stash, and probably a hall of infinity ones just like when Charles Kane made his last somber strides to infamy. My director will know how to tease out metaphor and the stubborn indulgence of subtext. And I guess I'll have to take up smoking Chesterfields, just as long as I don't have to stand outside in the cold for drags between snowflakes. Act Two should feature close-ups of things I distrust like time-released diet pills, my favorite soup pot after it boils dry, my tap shoes performing for guests in a childhood living room, oh and don't forget quick cuts of my elbow tattooed with an all-encompassing black & white spiral. And for the final scene, a 1940s bebop sax will be wailing, iced with my closing voice-over as I face a fourth wall. How to traffic through a moral clause as malleable as the wind blows. Just outside my window, tracks in the snow and the quiet glory of bright cardinals in branches.

Gift Shop at the Museum of Fear

The cashier will church you into the flavor of this place / maps to guide you through galleries of purple testaments, last stops in the vast design of things / It's okay to rattle grocery money when there are hermetically sealed jars of ghost heat, sour fog, incantatory rhythms, / under-the-bed cams / or dust-caked canteens with bullet holes for selfish mouths / signed copies of *The Doppelgänger's Guide for Arousing Am-I-Really-Who-I-Think-I-Am* / or postcard recipes from *The Cannibal's Cookbook* / It's okay to max out the plastic when there's a Roll-A-Top slot machine guaranteed to whisper your name all night / assorted lapel buttons like *I Survived Psychic Sweatshops* or *My Fear Engine Needs an Oil Change* / or wind-up toys that will howl in the wake of your scorched failures / So go ahead, rip off the cellophane and exit the building wearing your new PPE gear (with museum logos) for squirming through the next thick forest of tree thorns and brambles under a blood-and-smoke sky.

Black Moon, Gray Card

Gifts I would give you
        if I could: weekends
punctuated by playful accelerants
        like chuckles and chortles
from a rambunctious black moon,
        the ability to talk with
squirrels that visit your feeder
        to swap nutty aphorisms
and knock-knock jokes that prattle on
        over the speed limit, mood
ring that will only lighten your frame
        of mind, globe that will spin
you to wherever you imagine, gift
        card for all apologies and
thank-yous you never received,
        permission to be imperfect,
a feeling of peace so profound
        that your middle gray will
surrender to rainbow of pastels
        soothing you from solar
plexus to fingertips and toes.

Coin

A coin lands on its edge
and you remember your sad fingers
on the sprawled frog, still chilled
from the classroom refrigerator,
whose mission was to open its chest
and teach you about cardiac physiology.
You can't take back the cat who darted
across your early morning freeway ramp,
or the fawn whose last cries for its mother
stung your ears as you found it too late,
drowned and limp in the subdivision's
muddy ravine.

Each creature, an ambassador.
Martha, last passenger pigeon
now taxidermy-stuffed
in her own zoo memorial.
Sudan, last male
northern white rhinoceros
skinned and deboned,
headed for museum display.

A coin lands on its edge
and all it takes
is a vagrant breeze,
a slight vibration
to knock it over.
How many polar bear cubs
will fit in a Moses basket?
How many penguins
will continue in waddle or raft?
Obedient hound dogs
blood thick in backwoods,
bark into the brutal face
of night.

Last Offering

> *On 619/64 the last episode of Twilight Zone,*
> *"The Bewitching Pool" was broadcast on CBS.*

What can be bewitched—the ken of loneliness when a fish rots from the head. My womb swaying in an elevator's slow descent. A stuttering boy or girl making finger puppets in a snapdragon grove. The tripwire of belief. Sorrow of guilt. These children with their neurotransmitters of once-upon-a-time. Gap-toothed grins with feet of clay. Huck Finn treading surprise in the pool of their manicured grounds. Too much suburban bourbon over patio rocks. The mean crispness of capris with zipper teeth. These *junior citizens* swallow air on the bank of swimming hole where there's a way to pick their parents. Iced layer cake & white-haired crone hold court in gingerbread cottage while mothers & fathers evaporate in the cradle of memory. What souls relearn.

Art of Being Human
for Henry Bemis

Even you, page turner.
Even you, reader of condiment bottles
        and campaign buttons—back to your cage.
Even revulsion of truth to power.
Even preternatural buzz of conspiracy theory.
Even crosshairs of complicity.
Even lenses shattered and whispered regret.
Even *no country of mine.*
Even soot squalls of extinction.

Even substance in shadow.
Even clear water from kitchen tap,
        perfect snowflake on your tongue.
Even first gaze from new parent,
        rise and fall of huddled breaths.
Even slow rocking on front porch,
        warm slices of humming and
        hummingbird cake.
Even toes in cool clover,
        tender fingers entwined with
        wrinkled and dry.

Even long dreams woven
>   into rag rugs and afghans,
>   hot coffee under underpass,
>   wrapped sandwiches passed
>   from backpacks and car windows.

Even skies whose mission is to keep changing,
Even threads cut with your teeth,
Even tentative reconciliation,
Even narrow eyes of endpoint.
Even stark alone.
Even time enough.
Even this with courageous that.

Cento for His Monologues

excerpts from five seasons of Rod Serling's
opening and closing narrations

with many bromides applicable,
a collection of question marks
as they are wont to do in a very special bivouac area—
since this is strictly a story of make-believe
a strange province
a shadowland
small exercise in space psychology
not a virus, not a microbe, not a germ
not a good-natured counterman
not a gentle product in the form of a grandmother
or a twisted fanatic
or some rough-and-wooly nail-eaters
but proof positive that you can't out-punch machinery
in rebellion against the mechanics of our age
and the moment we forget this,
the ninety percent of the jigsaw pieces,
then we become the gravediggers
with the aggressive vinegar of a corpse
doomed to a perdition of unutterable loneliness
when fear that washes over

like fog and ocean spray—
yet you can find nobility and sacrifice,
no moral, no message, no prophetic tract
just a suit of armor held together by one bolt
call it faith
a naked target
like trying to pluck a note of music out of the air
and put it under glass to treasure,
that will-o'-the-wisp mirage that dangles
from the sky,
wishful thinkers made of glass
tormented by an imagination
sharp and pointed
as if some omniscient painter mixed a tube of oils
for some laughing ghosts that cross a mind
chasing an idol across the sand
and leave a second chance
lying in a heap
to shake hands figuratively
for a dark spot from the tapestry of life rubbed clean,
the genie you save may be your own
tilt-of-center,
going over the top of a rim—
let this be the postscript

EPISODE REFERENCES:

"Annoyed Aliens"
> "People are Alike All Over" (Season 1, Episode 25)
> "Mr. Dingle, the Strong" (Season 2, Episode 19)
> "Will the Real Martian Please Stand Up") (Season 2, Episode28)
> "To Serve Man" (Season 3, Episode 24)
> "Hocus-Pocus and Frisby" (Season 3, Episode 30)
> "Black Leather Jackets" (Season 5, Episode 18)
> "The Fear" (Season 5, Episode 35)

"The Art of Being Human"
> "Time Enough at Last" (Season 1, Episode 8)

"Black Moon, Gray Card"
> "The Big Tall Wish" (Season 1, Episode 7)
> "Little Girl Lost" (Season 3, Episode 26)

"Breach"
> "The Monsters Are Due on Maple Street" (Season 1, Episode 22)
> All quotes are from "He's Alive" (Season 4, Episode 4)

"Coin"
> "A Penny for Your Thoughts" (Season 2, Episode 6)
> "The Hunt" (Season 3, Episode 19)

"Consider"
> "Where is Everybody" (Season 1, Episode 1)
> "One for the Angels" (Season 1, Episode 2)
> "The Sixteen-Millimeter Shrine" (Season 1, Episode 4)
> "Static" (Season 2, Episode 20)
> "Kick the Can" (Season 3, Episode 21)
> "The Trade-Ins" (Season 3, Episode 31)
> "It's a Good Life" (Season 3, Episode 8)
> "Passage on the Lady Anne" (Season 4, Episode 17)
> "Ninety Years Without Slumbering" (Season 5, Episode 12)
> "Night Call" (Season 5, Episode 19)
> "Queen of the Nile" (Season 5, Episode 23)

"Crown of Cinquains for Women of Twilight Zone"
> "The Sixteen-Millimeter Shrine" (Season 1, Episode 4)
> "The Hitch-Hiker" (Season 1, Episode 16)
> "Mirror Image" (Season 1, Episode 21)
> "Eye of the Beholder" (Season 2, Episode 6)
> "The Invaders" (Season 2, Episode 15)

"Detours"
>"The Last Flight" (Season 1, Episode 18)
>"The Trouble with Templeton" (Season 2, Episode 9)
>"Back There" (Season 2, Episode 13)

"Enchanted Things"
>"The After Hours" (Season 1, Episode 34)
>"A Thing About Machines" (Season 2, Episode 4)
>"A Most Unusual Camera" (Season 2, Episode 10)
>"Long Distance Call" (Season 2, Episode 22)
>"The Mirror" (Season 3, Episode 6)
>"Dead Man's Shoes" (Season 3, Episode 18)
>"A Piano in the House" (Season 3, Episode 22)
>"Miniature" (Season 4, Episode 8)
>"Living Doll" (Season 5, Episode 6)

"Gift Shop at the Museum of Fear"
>"I Shot an Arrow into the Air" (Season 1, Episode 15)
>"The Fever" (Season 1, Episode 17)
>"The Purple Testament" (Season 1, Episode 19)
>"A World of Difference" (Season 1, Episode 23)
>"To Serve Man" (Season 3, Episode 24)

"How to Tame a Dream"
> "Perchance to Dream" (Season 1, Episode 9)
> "The Midnight Sun" (Season 3, Episode 10)
> "Shadow Play" (Season 2, Episode 26)

"In Which Obsolete Tries to Rewrite Its Story: The Last Episode"
> "The Mind and the Matter" (Season 2, Episode 27)
> "The Obsolete Man" (Season 2, Episode 29)
> "Phantom Camera"
> "Valley of the Shadow" (Season 4, Episode 3)
> "Poetry Accessories"
> "The Bard" (Season 4, Episode 18)
> "Some Crossword Clues"
> "Mr. Denton on Doomsday" (Season 1, Episode 3)
> "Showdown with Rance McGrew" (Season 3, Episode 20)

"Stopover"
> "Walking Distance" (Season 1, Episode 5)
> "Nightmare as a Child" (Season 1, Episode 29)
> "The Incredible World of Horace Ford" (Season 4, Episode 15)
> "Black Leather Jackets" (Season 5, Episode 18)

"Suburban Trajectory"
> "Deaths-Head Revisited" (Season 3, Episode 9)
> "Death Ship" (Season 4, Episode 6)

"Turkeys We Love"
> "Once Upon a Time" (Season 3, Episode 13)
> "Hocus-Pocus and Frisby" (Season 3, Episode 30)
> "Cavender is Coming" (Season 3, Episode 36)
> "From Agnes with Love" (Season 5, Episode 20)

"Twilight Ghazal"
> "And When the Sky Was Opened (Season 1, Episode 11)
> "What You Need" (Season 1, Episode 12)
> "The Four of Us Are Dying" (Season 1, Episode 13)

"Ventriloquist's Oath"
> "The Dummy" (Season 3, Episode 33)
> "Caesar and Me" (Season 5, Episode 28)

"Zones"
> "The Hitch-Hiker" (Season 1, Episode 16)
> "Living Doll" (Season 5, Episode 6)
> "The Masks" (Season 5, Episode 25)

Rikki Santer has worked as a journalist, a magazine and book editor, co-founder and managing editor of an alternative city newspaper in Cleveland, a poet-in-the schools, a high school teacher of English and film studies, and director of a student writing center. Currently she is serving as vice-president of the Ohio Poetry Association, an Ohio teaching artist through the Ohio Arts Council, and a member of the poetry troupe, Concrete Wink. With a M.A. degree in journalism from Kent State University and a M.F.A. degree in creative writing from The Ohio State University, her poetry has appeared in numerous publications both nationally and abroad. She has received many honors including five Pushcart and three Ohioana book award nominations as well as a fellowship from the National Endowment for the Humanities. *Stopover* is her 11th published poetry collection. Please contact her through her website: https://rikkisanter.com

www.ingramcontent.com/pod-product-compliance
Lightning Source LLC
Chambersburg PA
CBHW030137100526
44592CB00011B/928